THE WORLD'S TOP TEN

RIVERS

Neil Morris

Illustrated by Vanessa Card

Chrysalis Children's Books

Words in **bold** are explained in the glossary
on pages 30–31.

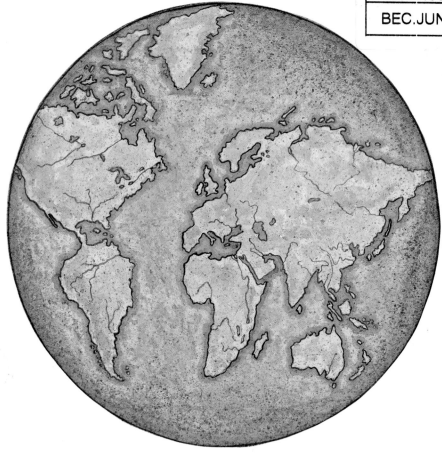

This edition published in 2003 by
Chrysalis Children's Books
The Chrysalis Building, Bramley Road,
London W10 6SP

Editor: Maria O'Neill
Designer: Dawn Apperley
Picture Researcher: Diana Morris
Consultant: Elizabeth M Lewis

Printed in China By Imago

Picture acknowledgements:
J Allan Cash: 14. Comstock: 25 top George Gerster. Eye
Ubiquitous: 5 bottom, 8, 9, 18, 29 bottom. Robert Harding
Picture Library: 10, 12, 13, 19, 28 bottom, 29 top. Hutchison
Library: 15. NHPA: 28 top. Russia and Republics Photo
Library: 27 Mark Wadlow. Still Pictures: 5 top, 11, 16 Bios, 21,
23, 26. Tony Stone Images: 22. Trip: 17, 20, 25 bottom.

ISBN 1 84138 487 9

British Library Cataloguing in Publication Data for this book
is available from the British Library.

Contents

What is a river?

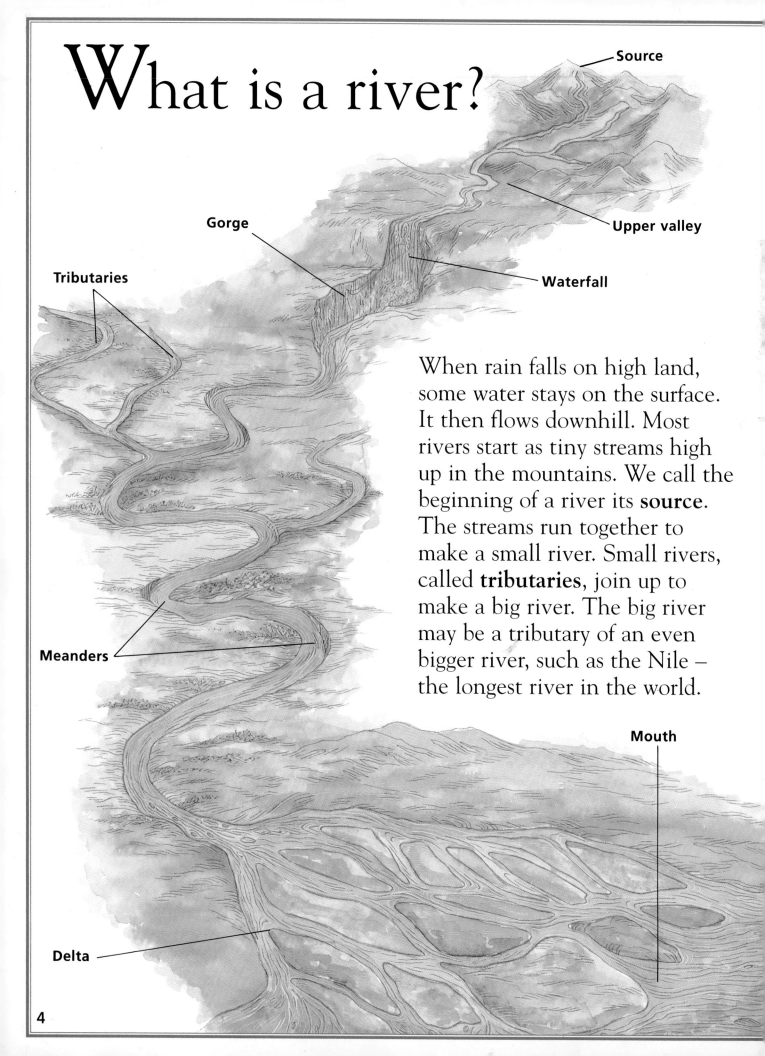

Source

Upper valley

Gorge

Waterfall

Tributaries

Meanders

Mouth

Delta

When rain falls on high land, some water stays on the surface. It then flows downhill. Most rivers start as tiny streams high up in the mountains. We call the beginning of a river its **source**. The streams run together to make a small river. Small rivers, called **tributaries**, join up to make a big river. The big river may be a tributary of an even bigger river, such as the Nile – the longest river in the world.

Flowing to the sea

As water flows, it wears the land away and makes a valley. A river carries with it a load made up of the soil and stones it has worn away. This moving load scrapes against the bottom and sides of the river bed, making it deeper and wider. This is how valleys are made by rivers, but it takes many thousands of years.

When a river is near its source it is narrow, shallow and fast. By the time it reaches the sea it seems to move more slowly. But, underneath, the flow of water is strong and dangerous. The end of the river is called its **mouth**.

A tributary of the River Po tumbles down the mountain side in Italy. As it flows towards the Adriatic Sea, it becomes wider and is dammed to make electricity.

Using rivers

People have always used the water from rivers to help them grow crops. They have also used rivers to travel by boat. Rivers were often the quickest way, or sometimes the only way, to cross large areas of unexplored land. Nowadays we build dams across rivers and use the power of flowing water to make **hydroelectricity**.

Rivers are so important that towns and cities throughout the world have grown up beside them. Today the **waste** from cities often pollutes the water.

Towns and villages lie along the banks of the Rhine, in Germany. Barges carry goods on the river. Nearby factories have caused **pollution**.

The longest rivers

In this book we take a look at the ten longest rivers in the world. We see how they have changed the landscape and affected the lives of the people who live near them.

The longest rivers

This map shows the ten longest rivers in the world. Long rivers have many tributaries. Each tributary has a different source and may have a different name from its main river. The main river and all its tributaries are called a **river system**. To find the length of a river, we measure from the source that is furthest from its mouth.

The world's top ten rivers

1	Nile	6670 km
2	Amazon	6448 km
3	Chang Jiang	6300 km
4	Mississippi	6020 km
5	Yenisei	5540 km
6	Huang He	5464 km
7	Ob	5409 km
8	Paraná	4880 km
9	Zaire	4700 km
10	Lena	4400 km

NORTH AMERICA

Mississippi

ATLANTIC OCEAN

Amazon

SOUTH AMERICA

PACIFIC OCEAN

Paraná

Nile

The Nile is the longest river in the world. Its water brings life to the desert countries that it flows through. Most of the people of Egypt live along its banks.

These Egyptian boats with triangular sails are called **feluccas**. They use the wind to sail up the Nile and travel back with the strong **current**.

Journey north

The Nile has two main branches. They are called the White Nile and the Blue Nile because of the different colours of their waters.

The White Nile begins as the River Kagera in the small African country of Burundi. It runs into Lake Victoria, the largest lake in Africa, and then heads north through **swamps** and deserts. At Khartoum, the capital of Sudan, the river is joined by the fast-flowing Blue Nile.

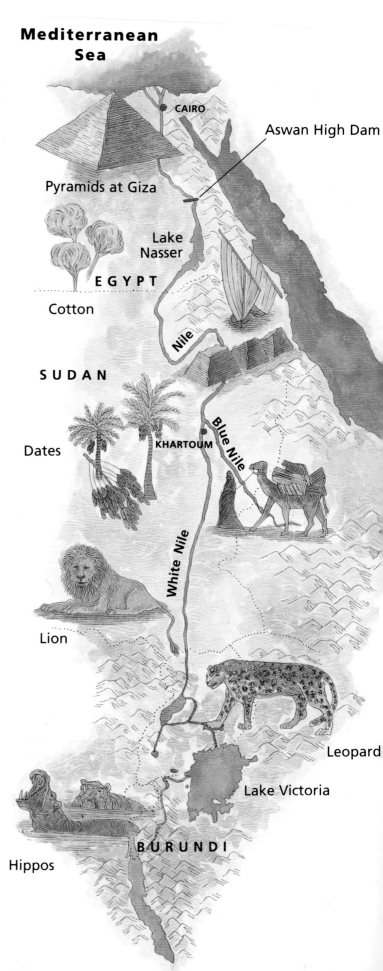

Mediterranean Sea

CAIRO

Aswan High Dam

Pyramids at Giza

Lake Nasser

EGYPT

Cotton

Nile

SUDAN

Dates

KHARTOUM

Blue Nile

White Nile

Lion

Leopard

Lake Victoria

BURUNDI

Hippos

FACTS

LENGTH   6670 km

SOURCE   Burundi,
central Africa

MOUTH   Egypt, into the
Mediterranean Sea

Land of the pharaohs

The Nile flows right through Egypt. Egypt's capital, Cairo, is built on the banks of the Nile, which flows on towards the Mediterranean Sea. The ancient Egyptians, whose kingdoms were ruled by **pharaohs**, worshipped the Nile.

They fished in it (see above), bathed in it, drank its waters and built tombs and temples on its shores. In ancient times, the river flooded every year. The floods spread **fertile** mud over the land, helping farmers to grow good crops.

A narrow canal has been dug next to the wide Nile to help water the land. Maize, wheat, rice and vegetables are important crops in Egypt, and cotton is grown to sell abroad.

Watering the desert

In modern times, people wanted to control the floods, and so dams were built across the Nile. The biggest; the Aswan High Dam, forms Lake Nasser. The lake is more than 500 kilometres long – which is nearly as long as England.

The lake stores flood water for use throughout the year, and the dam provides hydroelectricity. But it also stops fertile mud from moving downstream. This means that modern Egyptians have to use more chemicals to **fertilize** their land.

Amazon

The Amazon is not as long as the Nile, but it carries much more water. More than one fifth of all the water in the world's rivers flows down the Amazon.

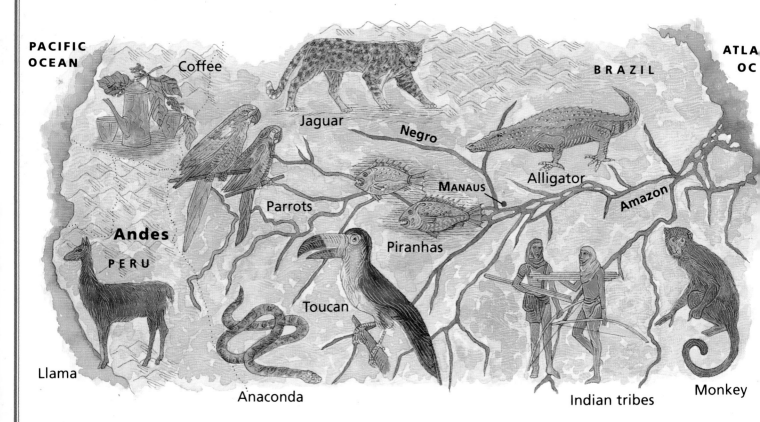

PACIFIC OCEAN

Coffee

Jaguar

Negro

BRAZIL

ATLA OC

Alligator

MANAUS

Amazon

Parrots

Piranhas

Andes

PERU

Toucan

Indian tribes

Monkey

Llama

Anaconda

Giant river system

The Amazon is fed by thousands of smaller rivers. By the time it reaches the sea, it is very wide. The Amazon **delta** is more than 300 kilometres across. In a single second it pours 200 000 cubic metres of water into the Atlantic Ocean. That is the same amount as held by a hundred Olympic-size swimming pools.

FACTS

LENGTH	6448 km
SOURCE	Lago Villafro, Peru
MOUTH	Brazil, into the Atlantic Ocean

The River Negro joins the Amazon near the city of Manaus. Manaus is an important centre of trade and one of Brazil's largest cities. A million people live there.

Melting snow in the Andes and tropical rain cause floods up to 9 metres deep in the Amazonian rain forest. The floods leave a water line high up on the trees.

Through the rain forest

The Amazon begins high in the Andes mountains of Peru. It flows across the plains of Brazil, through the biggest **tropical rain forest** in the world. Beside the river, parrots and toucans feed in the tree tops, while monkeys swing through the branches.

There are more than 2000 types of fish in the Amazon, from the bright angelfish to the deadly piranha with its razor-sharp teeth. Jaguars hunt by the river banks, while alligators and snakes swim in search of prey.

Many rivers flood when there is very heavy rain or when snow melts near the river's source. Every year the Amazon floods its vast rain forest.

Amazonian people

Hundreds of years ago many Indian tribal groups lived in villages along the Amazon. They ate food from the forest and fished in the river. But whole tribes were wiped out when huge areas of forest were cut down for wood, or burned to make way for crops and cattle ranches. Many people are now trying to save the Amazon rain forest.

Chang Jiang

In Chinese, Chang Jiang means 'long river'. The River Chang Jiang is called this because it is the longest river in China and the third longest river in the world.

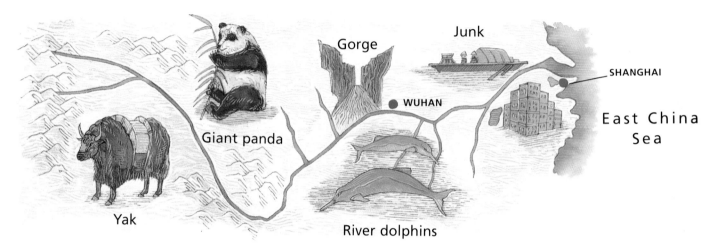

Gorge

Junk

SHANGHAI

WUHAN

East China Sea

Giant panda

Yak

River dolphins

Across China

The Chang Jiang is sometimes called the Yangtze. It begins high in the snow-covered mountains of western China. When the snow melts in summer, water trickles down to the **foothills** and forms streams. The streams then run together to make a river.

More than 700 small rivers join the Chang Jiang on its journey across China. At first the river passes through narrow **gorges**. Then it becomes wider as it moves over flat land. Finally the river flows into the East China Sea near Shanghai, China's largest city.

The Xiling Gorge is 76 kilometres long. The river zigzags through the gorge towards one of China's biggest dams, the Gezhouba.

A four-decker ferry carries people between Shanghai and the city of Chongqing. There are always many ships on the Chang Jiang near the port of Shanghai. They come here from all over the world.

FACTS

LENGTH   6300 km

SOURCE   Kunlun Mountains,
                western China

MOUTH   Eastern China, into the
                East China Sea

Using the river

Where the Chang Jiang rushes through gorges, the Chinese have built dams to turn the water's power into hydroelectricity. Between the city of Wuhan and the sea, the river is wide and deep enough for big ocean liners. But ferry boats, barges and rafts make up most of the river traffic.

People and animals

Nearly half of China's people live near the banks of the Chang Jiang. The river has plenty of fish and is home to dolphins and alligators. **Reserves** have been set up to protect the whitefin river dolphin, but there are probably only a few hundred alligators left in the lower part of the river.

13

Mississippi

The Mississippi, in America, forms the fourth longest river system in the world, with its main tributary, the Missouri.

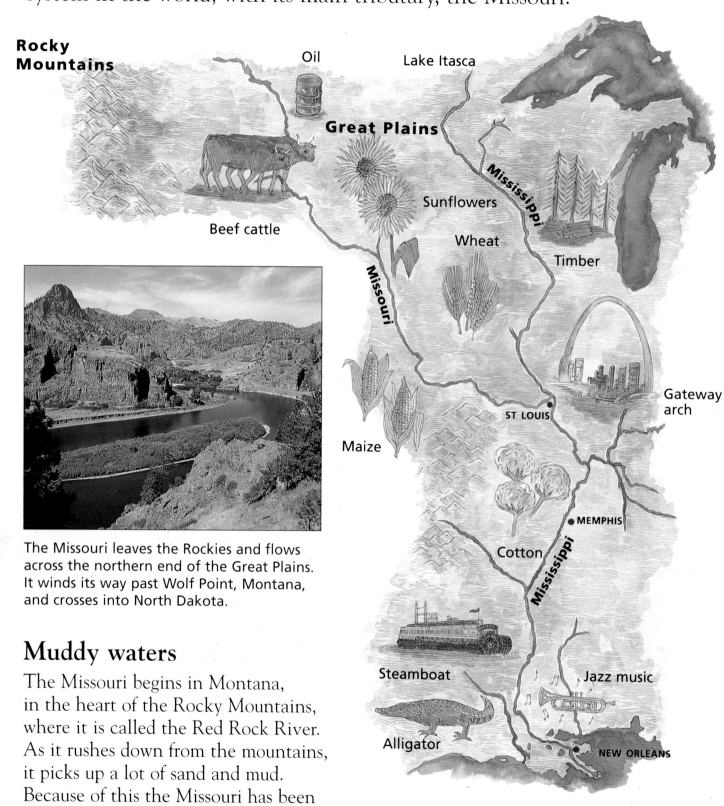

Rocky Mountains

Oil

Lake Itasca

Great Plains

Sunflowers

Beef cattle

Wheat

Mississippi

Missouri

Timber

Maize

ST LOUIS

Gateway arch

Cotton

MEMPHIS

Mississippi

Steamboat

Jazz music

Alligator

NEW ORLEANS

Gulf of Mexico

The Missouri leaves the Rockies and flows across the northern end of the Great Plains. It winds its way past Wolf Point, Montana, and crosses into North Dakota.

Muddy waters

The Missouri begins in Montana, in the heart of the Rocky Mountains, where it is called the Red Rock River. As it rushes down from the mountains, it picks up a lot of sand and mud. Because of this the Missouri has been given the nickname 'Big Muddy'.

Steamboat river

The source of the Mississippi is near Lake Itasca, Minnesota. In the language of local Indian tribes, Mississippi means 'great river'. It flows through the central lowlands of the United States, heading south towards the Gulf of Mexico.

Steamboats started taking goods and passengers up and down the river in 1812. Today the river is still an important route for carrying cargo. Tourists can also travel on the world's largest river boat, the *Mississippi Queen*, which is 116 metres long.

Danger from floods

The Missouri pours into the Mississippi just north of the city of St Louis. The river then winds on past Memphis, heading for New Orleans. At this point the river still has about 180 kilometres to go before it reaches the ocean.

In many places people have built high **embankments**, to stop the river from flooding. But in 1993 the worst flood in American history left more than 70 000 families homeless. Houses that were normally 6 kilometres away from the Mississippi disappeared under 5 metres of water.

The Mississippi flows through New Orleans. This modern city is one of the busiest ports in the world. Ships carry goods such as grain, paper, cotton, iron and steel.

FACTS

LENGTH	6020 km
SOURCE	Montana, USA
MOUTH	Louisiana, USA, into the Gulf of Mexico

15

Yenisei

The Yenisei is the longest of three big Siberian rivers. It flows from the south of Russia to its northern coast on the Arctic Ocean.

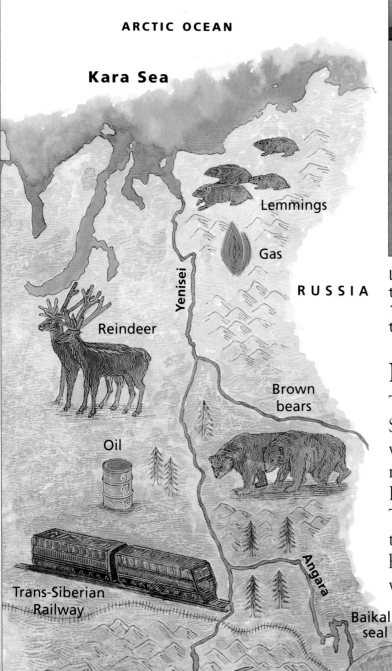

ARCTIC OCEAN

Kara Sea

Lemmings

Gas

RUSSIA

Yenisei

Reindeer

Brown bears

Oil

Angara

Trans-Siberian Railway

Baikal seal

Fish

Gold

Lake Baikal

MONGOLIA

Lake Baikal is frozen by mid-winter. People fish through holes in the ice, which is more than 1.5 metres thick in places. The lake is home to the world's only freshwater seal.

Deepest lake

The Yenisei begins as the River Selenga, near the Russian border with Mongolia. Along with 335 other rivers, the Selenga flows into Lake Baikal, the deepest lake in the world. This lake holds about one-fifth of all the fresh water on Earth. Lake Baikal has only one outlet, the River Angara, which flows into the Yenisei.

Forest and desert

The Yenisei runs north through Siberia, a vast region of Russia. For most of its journey it crosses the **taiga**, where reindeer graze (see above). This huge, cold forest is full of evergreen trees, such as fir, pine and larch. But a few hundred kilometres from the Arctic Ocean, the landscape changes. This is the **tundra**, an Arctic desert where the earth is always frozen. Only the top few centimetres thaw in summer and it is too cold for trees to grow.

FACTS

LENGTH	5540 km
SOURCE	Mongolia–Russia border
MOUTH	Russia, into the Kara Sea and the Arctic Ocean

Oil and minerals

There are many dams on the Yenisei, which make hydroelectricity. This is used to power **steel foundries** and **engineering plants**. Oil and gas have been found in the region. In 1994 there were large oil spillages that polluted Siberian rivers and caused damage to the environment. Gold, silver and other precious metals are also mined here.

The Yenisei is 300 kilometres south of the Arctic Circle as it flows past this village, which has sprung up between the taiga and the river.

Huang He

The Huang He is the second longest river in China, and the sixth longest in the world. Its name means 'Yellow River'. This comes from its muddy yellow colour. The Huang He is the world's muddiest river.

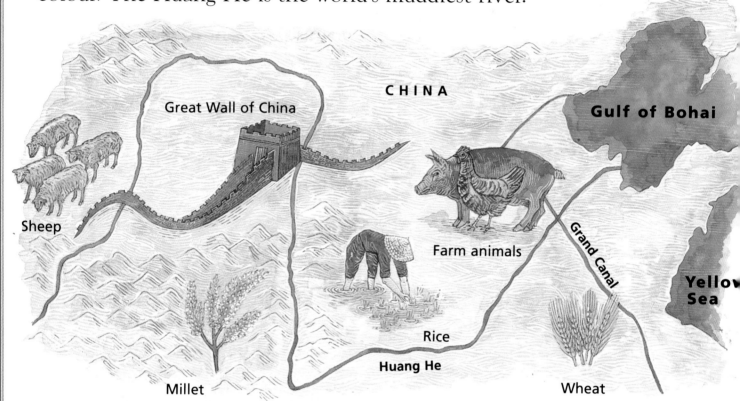

Sheep

Great Wall of China

CHINA

Gulf of Bohai

Farm animals

Grand Canal

Yellow Sea

Rice

Huang He

Millet

Wheat

Farming along the river

The Huang He begins on a high **plateau** and flows right across China to the Gulf of Bohai. The soil around the Huang He is made fertile by the river's muddy **silt**. This makes it ideal farming land, and Chinese civilization began here, about 9000 years ago.

Today the main crops are **cereals**, such as wheat, millet and rice. China is the world's greatest producer of wheat and rice, and more than two-thirds of Chinese people work on the land.

As the Huang He flows through the mountains, land on one side has been **cultivated** for crops.

Boats called junks carry goods on the Huang He. It is easy to see why the muddiest river in the world is called the Yellow River.

FACTS

LENGTH	5464 km
SOURCE	Qinghai province, western China
MOUTH	Eastern China, into the Gulf of Bohai and the Yellow Sea

People in danger

More than 100 million people live along the Huang He and its tributaries. In some places the river is higher than the surrounding countryside. People have built **dykes** to hold back the water, but the **plains** are easily flooded. Over the centuries, millions of people have been killed by floods, and the river is often called 'China's sorrow'.

Changing course

The Huang He has changed its course many times during its history. At different times it has poured into the Yellow Sea at points as far apart as 800 kilometres.

The Huang He is linked to the Chang Jiang by the Grand Canal (see above). This famous man-made waterway was begun before 500 BC, and work on it continued for hundreds of years.

Ob

The Ob is the second longest Siberian river when it is measured from the source of its greatest tributary, the Irtysh.

In winter the River Ob freezes over as far south as Novosibirsk, where these boats are moored.

The big freeze

The Irtysh begins on the border between China and Mongolia. It runs through Kazakhstan, into Russia, and then flows into the Ob on its way to the Arctic. The entire length of the River Ob is frozen solid each winter. Its **estuary** is blocked with ice from October to June. But in summer the river is an important route for ships carrying grain and cattle.

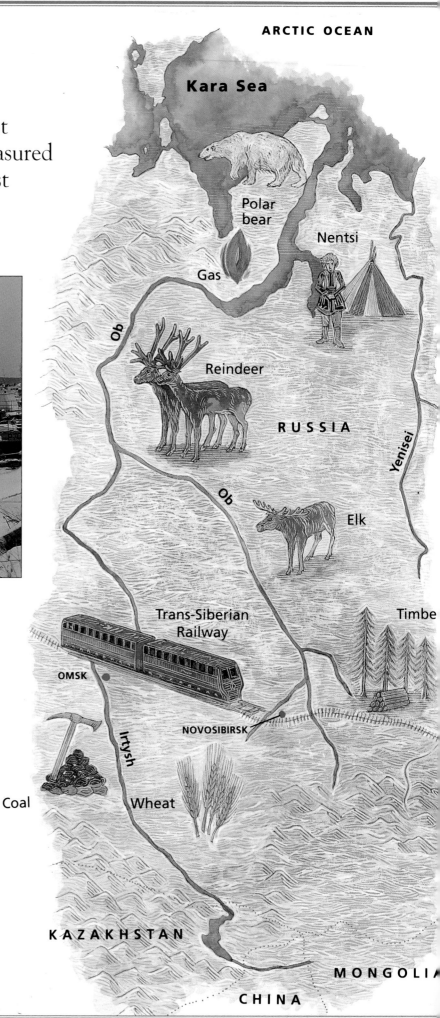

ARCTIC OCEAN

Kara Sea

Polar bear

Nentsi

Gas

Ob

Reindeer

RUSSIA

Yenisei

Ob

Elk

Trans-Siberian Railway

Timbe

OMSK

NOVOSIBIRSK

Coal

Irtysh

Wheat

KAZAKHSTAN

MONGOLIA

CHINA

Railway cities

The largest city in Siberia lies on the Ob. It is called Novosibirsk, and grew when the Trans-Siberian Railway was built in 1893. Almost one and a half million people now live in the city. The railway bridge over the Ob is the longest on the line. This famous railway connects Novosibirsk to the biggest city on the River Irtysh, which is called Omsk.

Traditional life

The Khanti and Mansi are two related peoples who live near the River Ob. Traditionally they went hunting in winter. In the summer they returned to their villages by the river, to fish. Now many of these people work on farms or in factories.

The Nentsi people live further north. They herd reindeer, hunt and fish. Many live in wigwams, but these are now covered with **tarpaulin** rather than fur and birch bark.

A Nentsi family in front of their wigwam. These people move around the Siberian tundra and forest, but many have now settled in farming villages.

FACTS

LENGTH	5409 km
SOURCE	China–Mongolia border
MOUTH	Russia, into the Kara Sea and the Arctic Ocean

Paraná

The Paraná is South America's second longest river, after the Amazon. It begins in south-eastern Brazil as the Paranáiba, and flows south into the Atlantic Ocean.

Country borders

In Brazil, the Paranáiba joins the Rio Grande to form the River Paraná. The Paraná is a border river. Travelling south, it forms the border between Brazil and Paraguay. Then it becomes the border between Paraguay and Argentina. After flowing through part of Argentina and past the city of Paraná, the river ends at the border between Argentina and Uruguay.

Just before the River Iguaçu joins the Paraná, water cascades 93 metres over the Paraná Plateau. The spectacular Iguaçu Falls are 4 kilometres wide.

PARAGUAY

Coffee

Football

Toucan

Rain forest

BRAZIL

Cattle

Itaipú Dam

Iguaçu

Cotton

Paraná

Iguaçu Falls

Tobacco

Paraná

Peanuts

Sheep

● PARANÁ

Armadillo

URUGUAY

ARGENTINA

Tourism

MONTEVIDEO

● BUENOS AIRES

Rio de la Plata

ATLANTIC OCEAN

Surge of power

In 1991 the world's biggest dam began making electricity on the upper part of the River Paraná. The concrete dam is called Itaipú, which means 'stone that sings'. It took 40 000 people 17 years to build. The dam is on the border between Brazil and Paraguay. Both countries paid for and share the dam's electricity.

Water plunges through the Itaipú dam. The river's power drives **generators** to make electricity.

River of silver

Near the end of its journey, the Paraná flows past the grassy plains called **pampas**. Here **gauchos** herd their cattle. As it reaches the Atlantic, the river flows into a huge estuary called Rio de la Plata, which means 'river of silver'. Millions of people live on the shores of the estuary. Montevideo, the capital of Uruguay, is on the northern shore, and Buenos Aires, the capital of Argentina, lies to the south. The mouth of the estuary is 225 kilometres wide.

FACTS

LENGTH	4880 km
SOURCE	South-east Brazil
MOUTH	Rio de la Plata, Argentina and Uruguay, into the Atlantic Ocean

Zaire

The Zaire is the second longest river in Africa, after the Nile. Unlike the Nile, the Zaire flows through tropical rain forest and grassland. It crosses the **Equator** twice as it heads west towards the Atlantic Ocean.

Monkey

Boyoma Falls

CONGO

EQUATOR

Zaire (Congo)

Hornbill

Fish

Crocodile

Hippos

ZAIRE

Gorilla

Rain forest

Mangrove swamp

ATLANTIC OCEAN

ANGOLA

Parrot

Python

Lualaba

ZAMBIA

Zaire or Congo

The Zaire begins as the Lualaba near the border between Zaire and Zambia. It flows north and crosses the Equator just before the great Boyoma Falls. More water flows over the Boyoma Falls than over any other waterfall in the world. The River Zaire flows on through thick forest towards the country of Congo. For about 600 kilometres the river forms the border between Zaire and Congo. The Zairians call the river the Zaire, and the Congolese call it the Congo.

FACTS

LENGTH	4700 km
SOURCE	Zaire–Zambia border, southern Africa
MOUTH	Zaire–Angola border, into the Atlantic Ocean

The Zaire has many **rapids** and waterfalls, both at the beginning and the end of its journey to the ocean. Ships can travel on the river for just over a third of its length.

Exploring the river

In 1874 an explorer named Henry Morton Stanley began a journey down the Zaire. It took him nearly three years. At that time the people of the region were native Africans, mainly Bantu and Pygmies. When the Europeans arrived, they took over the land and ruled the local people. Zaire and Congo became independent countries in 1960.

Fishermen use rapids to catch the river's fish in baskets tied on the end of long poles.

Home of the hippo

Herds of hippopotamuses lie submerged in the river. At some places along its banks, the rain forest creeps right up to the water's edge. Gorillas, monkeys, parrots, hornbills, pythons and vipers all live here.

Lena

The third longest Siberian river, the Lena, is the tenth longest river in the world. It begins as the River Kirenga near Lake Baikal and flows north to the Arctic Ocean.

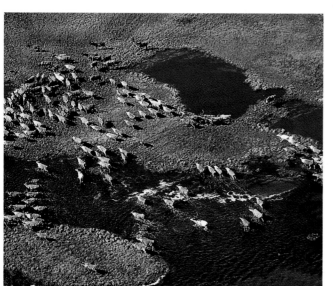

Reindeer **migrate** between summer breeding grounds on the tundra and winter feeding grounds in the forests further south. Yakut herdsmen move with the reindeer.

Yakut people

The Yakuts live on the Central Siberian Plateau, beside the River Lena. Here the summers are short and the winter temperatures are some of the coldest on Earth, at -50°C and even colder. The Yakuts herd reindeer. Some people still live in traditional wooden houses or log huts. But during the long winter, many now prefer to live in apartment blocks in the city of Yakutsk.

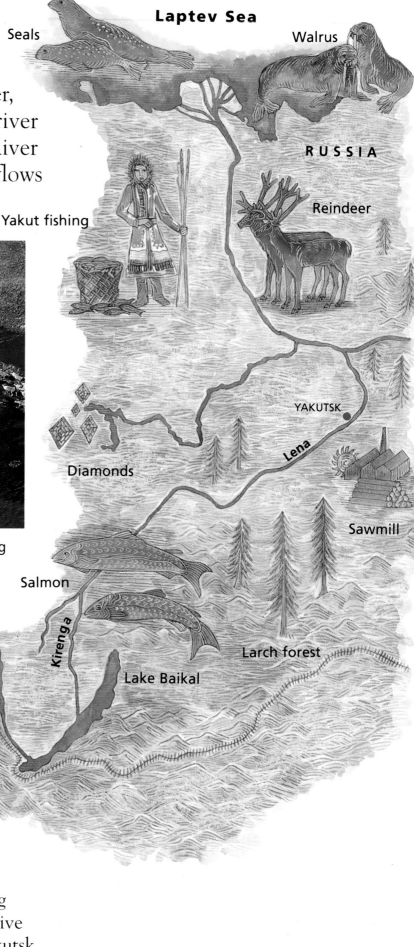

Laptev Sea

Seals

Walrus

RUSSIA

Reindeer

Yakut fishing

YAKUTSK

Lena

Diamonds

Sawmill

Salmon

Kirenga

Larch forest

Lake Baikal

FACTS	
LENGTH	4400 km
SOURCE	Near Lake Baikal, Russia
MOUTH	Russia, into the Laptev Sea and the Arctic Ocean

Sawmill city

There are huge areas of larch forest on the slopes surrounding the Lena. Yakutsk grew up as a sawmill city, using the river to transport timber. For a long time only wooden houses were built in the city. Now large concrete pillars are driven into the frozen soil so that apartment blocks and other buildings can be put up.

The river grows wider as it flows across the plains of the Yakut region of Russia. There are pillars of rock here that are as tall as trees.

Siberian animals

Like other Siberian rivers, the Lena has plenty of salmon, sturgeon and other fish. The river pours into the Laptev Sea through a wide delta, and this is home to walruses and seals. Polar bears also roam the frozen Arctic ice in search of their favourite prey, ringed seals.

The world's rivers

Five of the world's ten longest rivers flow through Asia, the biggest continent. Two of them are in Africa, another two in South America, and one in North America. But there are important rivers on the other continents too.

Murray-Darling

The Murray is the longest river on the continent of Australia. From the source of its biggest tributary, the Darling, to its mouth in the Indian Ocean, it is 3750 kilometres long. This great river system provides fertile farming land and is used to make hydroelectricity. It winds its way through forests of eucalyptus trees (see right).

Thames

The River Thames is the second longest river in the United Kingdom after the Severn. Its source is in the Cotswold Hills in the south of England. The Thames flows through London, passing the Houses of Parliament and the Tower of London. It also passes under many bridges, which can cause a problem for ships coming in from the North Sea. A famous bridge called Tower Bridge solves this problem by opening in the middle and swinging up in the air to let ships through. It was built in 1894. The Thames is 346 kilometres long, so the Nile is almost 20 times longer!

Colorado

Rivers change the landscape by carving out patterns for themselves. The Colorado River, in the USA, has dug deep gorges and created amazing sets of **meanders**. This one, in Arizona, is called Horseshoe Bend. The Colorado River rises in the Rockies. It flows for 2320 kilometres, through Colorado, Utah and Arizona to the Gulf of California in Mexico. Over millions of years it has carved out the largest gorge in the world. The Grand Canyon is 1.6 kilometres deep, up to 29 kilometres wide, and is 446 kilometres long.

Ganges

Rivers can be holy places. The River Ganges is holy to all followers of the Hindu religion. To them the river is Ganga Mai, or 'Mother Ganges'. Every year, about a million Hindus go to the Indian city of Varanasi to bathe in the river. They believe its water will wash away their sins.

The Ganges starts 3000 metres high in the Himalaya Mountains, the world's highest mountain range. Here it is fed by the melting snows. It flows across northern India into Bangladesh, finally emptying into the Bay of Bengal. About 200 million people live in the valley of the Ganges, which is 2510 kilometres long.

Glossary

cereals Grasses that produce grains we can eat, such as wheat.

cultivate To prepare land for crops.

current A strong, steady flow of water in one direction.

delta The fan-shaped area at the mouth of some rivers, where the main flow splits up into many smaller channels.

dyke A bank of earth or other material, built to stop a river from flooding.

embankment A bank of earth or stone that acts as a dyke.

engineering plant A factory where machines and tools are made.

Ancient Egyptians fishing in the Nile.

A gaucho riding on the Argentinian pampas.

Equator An imaginary circle around the middle of the Earth.

estuary The wide part of a river at its mouth, where the river's fresh water mixes with the sea's salt water.

felucca A boat with triangular sails.

fertile Land that is fertile has rich soil and produces good crops.

fertilize To make fertile.

foothills The lower slopes of a mountain.

gaucho A cowboy and cattleman from Argentina.

generator A machine that turns one form of energy, such as the power of water, into electricity.

gorge A steep, rocky, narrow pass. A river may run through it.

hydroelectricity Electric power made by the force of moving water.

meander A curve or bend in a river.

migrate To travel from one place to another at particular times of the year.

mouth The end of a river, where it flows into the sea.

pampas The grassy plains of Argentina.

pharaoh An ancient Egyptian king.

plain Flat countryside without many trees growing on it.

plateau A flat area of high land.

pollution Damage caused by poisonous and harmful substances.

rain forest Thick forest found in warm tropical areas of heavy rainfall.

rapids Part of a river where the water moves very fast over rocks.

reserve An area set aside for the protection of animals.

river system A large river and all the smaller rivers that flow into it.

Reindeer grazing in the taiga.

silt A fine layer of mud and clay.

source The place where a river begins.

steel foundry A factory where steel is made and cast into shapes.

swamp An area of marshy ground.

taiga Cold Arctic forest of evergreen trees, such as pine and larch.

tarpaulin A thick waterproof sheet, often made of canvas and then coated with tar.

tributary A small river that flows into a larger one.

tropical Found in the tropics. The tropics are near the Equator. They are the hottest part of the Earth.

tundra Flat treeless plains of the Arctic regions, where the earth is always frozen beneath the surface.

waste Rubbish, sewage, unwanted and sometimes harmful substances produced by people, both at home and at work.

Hippos wallowing in a river.

Index

Words in **bold** appear in the glossary on page 31.